A Boyfriends Guide to Being Affectionate

Table of Contents

Introduction

I want to thank you and congratulate you for purchasing the book "A Boyfriends Guide to Being Affectionate"

This book contains proven steps and strategies on how to become a truly romantic and loving boyfriend who cares about the girl so much. It tells you how to win her heart with your everyday actions and sweet affection.

Here's an inescapable fact: you will need to know how to respect her and how to treat her as another half to give her your affection in the most loving way. The book comes with different chapters that focus on different aspects of being affectionate.

If you do not develop your way in which you love and care for her, she could move on from the relationship and find another worthy person who deserve to have her in his life.

It's time for you to become an amazing boyfriend who showers her with complete attention and abundance of affection. It is time for you to make her completely yours by sweeping her off her feet with your utmost love and care.

Chapter 1: The art of respecting your girl

Picking up a girl is easier nowadays, but a man should always know how to treat her and respect her if he wants to keep her throughout his life. The first and foremost point to remember is to be completely honest with respect and a bit of playfulness to keep the relationship pure and joyous.

Every woman deserves to be loved and respected for who she is and she should have the freedom and comfort with a man to keep the relationship healthy and long lasting. The core of a relationship gets sturdier when you treat her with the respect she deserves and she will definitely love you back for the man you are.

Some tips on how to treat her with respect are:

- You should be honest and direct

- You should respect and admire her smartness

- You should listen to the things she says and remember it

- You should give her some of your attention at times

- You should be a caring gentleman

- You should give her space and respect her boundaries

- You should be confident and fearless when you are with her

Being honest and direct:

Honesty is always vital in any relationship. It builds trust and it gives meaning and strength to the relation between two souls. In a romantic relationship with a girl, always telling the truth can be tough, but you must remember that it is not healthy to take the easy route by lying.

If you get caught with your lie, then things can go worse and it can put an enormous amount of stress in the relationship you share with your girl. The essential part of respecting her is by being honest and straight to her even about the smallest things in life.

You have to understand that it is better to tell the truth rather than lying in the long run of a relationship. Keeping up with all your lies and protecting it can be stressful and it can ruin a relationship when she finds out.

Respecting and admiring her smartness:

If you can give out your thoughts and opinions in life, then she should deserve the same thing too. It is okay to have differences in opinion, but you should know how to treat her and her opinions. You should never have the egoistic mind of thinking that your opinions are stronger and better than hers.

If she has a very different opinion on subjects like arts and literature, you should have the decency to listen the explanation of why she thinks that way. You can get into a deep logical debate with her explanation, but it is vital that you acknowledge and respect her perspective in all those things. After all, the difference of opinion comes from the varying life experience each person goes through. You should not take that difference personally.

Listening to her and remembering the things she says:

One obvious way to show your girlfriend that you value her and take her seriously with respect is by listening to her when she is speaking. Keep her engaged in a conversation by responding to her with your own thoughts.

You should also remember all those important conversations which revealed her hidden and true identity with all her courage. You need not remember all the things that she says, but make sure that you remember the most important things that she says to you. This will show her that you completely value and respect her thoughts with care.

Giving her the attention at times:

You and your girlfriend should never compete and thrive for each other's attention. Show your respect and love by being attentive towards her when you are with her.

If you take her out on a date, she should be your first priority and you should give her all your attention at that time. When she comes over to your place to meet you and spend some time with you, you must acknowledge the reason she is there and you should give her the attention she deserves. Spend time with her when you are with her and that is how you should treat her.

Being a caring gentleman:

You should develop your character and personality to be a gentleman around women. And if she is your girlfriend, you should show the essence of gentleness more with lots of care and love.

Pull out the chair when she sits down at a restaurant. Hold the door at times and pay for the dinner date at times without sharing. You need not do it all the time, but you should have it in you to be a gentleman at times to let her know that she is special. Ask her if she is comfortable with these things and if she is not, just let her be and embrace the freedom from doing all these things. You need not display the formal etiquette if she is a casual woman who doesn't care about these things.

Giving her space and respecting the boundaries:

You should be smart enough to respect her boundaries because her idea about some behaviors might be difference from yours. If she finds it uncomfortable to make out in a public place, then don't put her in that situation. It can end in a conflict later on.

She might be naturally shy about all these things and you should never be ignorant about this difference in opinions and her feelings. You should stop yourself from doing such things that put her out of the comfort zone. Think about it and try to understand them in her perspective to have a smooth and healthy relationship.

Being confident and fearless when you are with her:

Be your own self with all your courage and do not be afraid to share the deepest and scariest secrets of yours. This is another way of showing your respect towards her. Be open to her and do not feel scared to express your feelings, be it good or bad.

Open your heart out to her and express all your inner fears and doubts that make you who you are. Tell her about your worries and ask for her opinion on these things. You can keep the stress out by talking out to her about the things that worry you. After all, that is why she is there for you.

Thus, the integral strength of a relationship comes from respecting her and her values when you are with her. You must never give in to your manly ego and refrain yourself from giving the respect she deserves. When you respect your girlfriend and treat her the way she deserves to be treated, she would obviously feel the genuine affection you have towards her. You need not try hard to show it in any other way.

Chapter 2: How to care for her

You should know how to care for her when she is in a serious relationship with you. Caring for her and being kind is a great sign of a healthy affection towards her. She will feel special and she will love spending her time with you when you care for her from the bottom of your heart.

So, if you want to show her that you truly care for her with all your heart, you must follow the tips given below:

- Be sharp and proactive in the relationship

- Try to keep in touch with her at times

- Avoid being materialistic

- Do random and sweet things to cheer her up

- Try to be your own self when you are with her

- Make her realize that she is a valuable person in your life

Being sharp and proactive:

Like all the girls, even your girl would not want to ask you to be treated nice. She might want you to do it at your own wish spontaneously. Do things that make her feel good even before she asks for it.

Hold on to her hands while you take a walk, listen to her with your complete attention when she talks, look her deep into the eyes when she says important things, remember her birthday and your anniversary. These small things would make her feel loved and cared for. This is vital because it will keep her at bay from feeling lonely and needy. Do all these out of respect and love.

Keeping in touch with her at times:

It is unhealthy for a relationship if you talk to her only once in a blue moon. She should be able to feel your presence at times and you should do this by keeping in touch with her. Some couples might have a very different kind of relationship, but you should meet her at least once a week and text her or call her at times. You should know if she doing fine and happy.

You should have the natural urge to do these things. Ask her about her day at the end of the day and ask her about the troubles she tackled throughout the week at work/college. You should contact her on your own and shouldn't just stick on to responding to her calls and texts. Take the first step and try to initiate a conversation once in a while.

Not being materialistic:

It is not really romantic if you consider money and possessions to be important than her. And if she finds out that with the way you behave, she might as well leave you to end the relationship. You should always consider her over any other materialistic desires.

For example, when she is sad and wants you to talk, you should be in the position to talk to her and make her feel good. It won't be good if you carry on with your work or pleasure when she is in a bad mood. You should keep her life in perspective before all the things that makes you rich in the materialistic sense. You should cherish real love and embrace the eternal joy it provides.

Doing random and sweet things to cheer her up:

Every normal boyfriend would treat his girlfriend well and care for her by celebrating big and important days like birthdays, special holidays and anniversaries. But you should get over that normalcy and be an exceptional boyfriend by showing her that you care for her even on other normal days.

Take her out as a surprise when she doesn't expect it. Give her a love note with a short and sweet poem about her. Present her a rose on a beautiful sunny day. Send her a sweet and loving text message from your heart. The things that you do might not be big, but it will be sweet and it will make her swoon with your love and affection. These little things showcase that you really care for her and think about her all the time.

Being your own self with her:

This should be an essential aspect of a healthy relationship. You should always strive to be yourself when you are with her and this should be mutual between you both. You should be able to show your real inner self and none of the other characters that you pretend to be at times.

Be truthful and honest about the negative emotions that run in your mind. Express it to her and be open about these kinds of emotions. Show the real part of you without hiding anything. And acknowledge that she is also a part of you like you are a part of her in the relationship.

Making her realize her own value in your life:

This is a sensitive aspect to look after, because it goes beyond all your sweet compliments and lovely surprises. Compliments and surprises can become boring and dull as the days go by in a relationship. But she must know that you consider her as an important person in life.

Show her your true inner side and tell her about the things that hurt you and make you feel sad. Go to her for comfort when you feel bad and hurt. Try to remember the details of the things that make her lovely and beautiful. And compliment her with those things that make her special and unique from everyone else.

These are the ways by which you can show your caring and kind heart in a relationship. It is vital that you care for her all the time without expecting anything back. She will eventually love you and enjoy your presence for who you are and she would be proud to have you in her life.

Chapter 3: Giving her a good time

You should always make sure that she has a good time with you. She should be able to tell about a thousand happy memories that make the relationship lovely and deep. Get out of your comfort zone and make her feel happy. Improvise on your imaginations and give her the best time when you are around her. Here are some tips to help you do that:

- Be smart with your date plans and ideas

- Dedicate a whole night for her

- Pay for her at times

- Praise her for who she is in the inner side

- Make her feel unique and special in your life

Being smart with date plans and ideas:

You need not follow the herd and follow the usual date plans like a movie night out or a fancy dinner at a restaurant. Get smart and be creative in this aspect. Try to do things with her that she would have never imagined that she would do in her life. Go out of your comfort zone and get her out of hers.

This will give you a great chance to bond so much closer as a couple. It can also save you some money if you are a young and adventurous couple. Do things that she wanted to do, but never had the chance or guts to do.

Dedicating a whole night for her without any distractions:

Plan a night for her and dedicate it completely for her. Do not spend time for other commitments or people on that night. Keep aside everything else in your life for those few hours. Clear your mind and heart to direct your complete attention towards her.

This will make the relationship stronger and she will feel that you are being the sweetest and affectionate guy ever. Turn off all your electronic devices like phone, PC, laptop and gaming consoles to spend that time with her. Never give in to distractions on that night. Make sure that the whole night is dedicated only for her and prove it by treating her that way.

Paying for her at times with complete respect:

You need not share the dinner bills all the time. Surprise her by paying for her if she is comfortable with it. If you plan the night for her, then make sure that it is on your expense.

Make her feel comfortable about the fact that money comes as a secondary thing when it comes to spending time with her. If she is not comfortable with you paying for her, you can just smile at her and compliment her for being awesome. You need not go into an argumentative mode at times like this to ruin her mood.

Making her feel unique and special in your life:

You must realize the fact that she is going to be the important person in your life. Make sure that she feels the same way about you by involving her into your depth of life. Talk to her about the adventures you want to experience with her and start a conversation about how your relationship can be after so many years.

Be frank and honest when you are expressing these things. You need not talk to her in an elegant and embellished language to make her feel that way. Be yourself and let her be herself. She will easily find out when you are not being yourself, so it is better to be open and raw.

Make a genuine offer to pay and ask her if you can. Do not do it out of the etiquette that has to be followed, instead do it like you want to do. If she insists on paying that night, improvise and settle a deal with her. Grab a coin and toss it to decide who has to pay. You need not do this all the time. You can always allow her to pay for your dinner at times. Keep this deal simple and casual. Do not spend so much of your time arguing about this issue and if she keeps on coming up with that argument, change the topic with your smartness.

Praising her for who she is:

Express your love for her by praising her for who she is underneath her beautiful body. Let your most passionate and deep expressions embrace her with warmth and love. Focus your compliments and praises on the things that make her who she is, like her smartness, humor sense, personality and so on. You don't have to praise her for her aesthetic beauty all the time.

Do not objectify her and don't put off the spark of the moment in a romantic situation. Make use of it and let her know about how deeply you love her. Say that you love her imperfections and the way they complete her.

True love and affection can be expressed effortlessly if you go over and beyond her normal expectations in a relationship. So put out your effort to:

Know her friends and family:

Try whatever you can to get along with the vibe of her friends and family members. Keep in mind that they are important persons in your girlfriend's life and you should have a similar opinion about them. This will make her feel that you respect her life and her circle. It is also a sign of seriousness in a relationship.

Plot a treasure hunt to excite her:

You can always do something fun to spend a day with her. Treasure hunt is an awesome and fun-filled choice.

- o Plan your treasure at first. Keep it light, like a piece of jewelry or a music CD.

- o Plan the whole structure of the treasure hunt. Decide the timing and plan the places to put your treasures at.

- o Use romantic clues that bring back old memories of your relationship.

- o Plan the notes accordingly and make sure the first note would be found by her obviously.

- Do not make it too difficult and hurt her brain. Keep it light and fun.

Cook her dinner:

You need not take her out on a date for dinner. You can cook her meal at your place and invite her for dinner. Do not worry a lot about messing up. She would really love it that you tried and thought about it. Keep the meal simple and light, so that it is easy for you to make and easy for her to eat. Make a balanced meal that is healthy and avoid serving a lot. Make sure that the dining area is clean and pretty when you serve her the dinner. Invest in a wine bottle for the night.

Prepare a CD mix for her:

Collect songs that are common to both of you and the songs that she loves. Memories can be greatly influenced with music and use that trait to attract her attention. If your voice is good, you can also pitch in a song in your own voice to surprise her. Create a romantic track list that is sweet and not so long.

Take her out for a picnic at times:

On a sunny afternoon, go ahead to her place and pick her up for a surprise picnic. Prepare a light lunch along with refreshing drinks for the picnic. Pick a spot where she loves to spend her time, like her favorite park or a view point in the hilltop.

Chapter 4: Everyday actions and surprises to make her happy

Your everyday actions and behaviors can tell a lot about you and show your affection towards your girlfriend. Do not fret and worry if you think you are not going a good job. Man up and change the way you treat her to make her feel loved.

Some of the everyday actions that can show your affection towards her:

Being direct:

You must never assume that she knows how you feel and think about her. She might even forget that you are thinking about her. Make sure that you tell her how you feel about her at times. Do not make her feel uncertain of your feelings about her. It can easily spoil the relationship in the long run.

Asking her about the day at night:

You are her partner. You should act and be like one if you want to keep her in your life. Listen to what she has to say about the day. Help her out in solving problems that she might face in the future. Be empathetic and open your ears to listen to her highs and lows in life. This is a definite bonding trait for a strong and healthy relationship.

Being patient and listening to her:

It is important that you listen to whatever she has to say with lots of patience. Even if it does not interest you, you must try hard to pay attention to what she has to say. Learn to read between the lines when she talks and offer to help her if you understand them.

Listening to her patiently will make her feel like that you care for her and her life. It will also strengthen the trust and love between you both. While listening, try to get involved in the chat but do not take over control.

Keeping the compliments light and heartfelt:

Compliment about the things that she knows are true about her. Let her know if she looks beautiful and charming on a particular day. Appreciate her new look if she gets a new haircut. Appreciate the way she works hard at college or work. Admire her way of dressing and compliment about the same.

Never stop trusting her:

Trust is an integral part of a healthy relationship. If you don't trust a person, they will never trust you back because they don't have to. Build a strong trust between you both and live on it.

If she is having a day out with her friends, do not check on her every few hours. Let her have some fun with her friends for that day. Do not be jealous when she talks to other guys. It also shows that you are not confident with the relationship you are sharing with her.

Being respectful even after a fight:

Do not let a silly fight or an argument to get into your egoistic mind. Be respectful even when you are angry. You should not shout and yell at her just because you are angry. If you have any problem with her, bring up a conversation about the problem only with her and not anyone else. Don't live on the past mistakes and use them against her when she is vulnerable.

Respect her smartness and do not assume that she needs help for doing all the things in life. Let her be independent when she wants to and give her the space to be herself. Avoid teasing her about her ideals and values. Never abuse her physically or verbally.

Sweet surprises to make her happy:

1. Make her happy with a short and sweet love note at times. It shows that you genuinely love her. Handwritten notes are even more romantic and personal. Avoid typing it down in a soft format and printing it out. The boring black fonts might never feel personal and romantic.

2. Keep saying that you love her. Do not feel shy to say it once you have explained your love. She will be expecting you to say it and make her feel happy by saying it.

3. Contact her and talk to her before going to bed. A tuck in call is a great way to show that you really care about her every day. Let her know that she is always in your mind. When you do this, you will be last person she thinks about before going to sleep.

4. Give her chocolates and sweet treats often. You need not get expensive Swiss chocolates to fulfil her cravings. Treat her with candies and bar chocolates time to time. Bake her some yummy Choco-chip cookies on your own. If she is not that into sweets, then go for a snack that she loves.

5. Surprise her with flowers when she is least expecting it. Drop it at her work

place or home. Make sure that the flowers are bright and vibrant to look at. Write a note along with the bouquet to make it extra special.

6. Choose a simple gift time to time. Surprise her with a small and cute gift on a dull day. Get her accessories that match her vibrant character and personality.

7. Be affectionate when she doesn't expect it. Be loving and sweet-talk after a fight or an argument. Make her feel good that you are the one fighting or arguing with her.

Chapter 5: Subtle ways of physical intimacy

A healthy and lovely relationship always has a part of a little bit of physical intimacy and closeness. It should be subtle and gentle so that it sparks the romance between you both instead of ruining it.

Here are some tips for you to do that:

1. Give a playful nudge at times when you are with her. Do not overdo and hurt her. Laugh at her when she tumbles on your nudging. Be comfortable around her and let her know that she can do the same things to you at times.

2. Kiss her on the top of her head to let her know that you love her. A kiss to the forehead is always sweet and it shows

that you really care for her. Do it at least once a day if you are living with her.

3. Rub the small of her back at times with your hand. Do it slowly and casually and let her enjoy the soothing effect it gives.

4. Keep your feet next to hers when you are relaxing with her. Play with her feet under the dinner table when you are dining. These actions can be cute and adorable.

5. Give her a romantic wink at times. A wink can induce a lovely effect on her. It is fun and she will never expect that. See her reaction after you wink and you will certainly get a wink back if you are lucky.

6. Snuggle and cuddle with her time to time. Do it when you two are sitting on a couch and watching television. Rest your head on her shoulders when you are done with the cuddling love.

7. This is a basic and essential way of being affectionate. Hold her hands while walking with her. It is a romantic sign and couples always look adorable when they hold their hands and walk down a street.

8. Give her random kisses when she least expects it. Unexpected kisses need not always be on the lips, you can choose to kiss the back of her neck. You can also kiss her hand or shoulder at times.

9. Give her a warm and comforting hug when she leaves you to work or college. An extra hug will always be appreciated and she will obviously love the warmth and scent that your hug provides.

10. When she is cold and numb, pull her close to you and keep her warm. Rub your hands and warm her cheeks if you have to.

There are a million ways to show your affection and your girlfriend would find it really sweet when you are affectionate towards her. Charm her and win her heart with your unconditional love and affection to make her yours for the lifetime.

Conclusion

Thank you again for downloading this book!

I hope this book was able to help you to be affectionate towards your girlfriend in all the ways possible. Being affectionate is a trait that all boyfriends should have and it is something every girlfriend deserves from her loved one.

The next step is to start being affectionate and shower her with all your love and warmth to make her the most special and happy girl in the world. When you do that, she is obviously going to treat you back with all her love and affection.

Thank you and good luck!

Made in the USA
Middletown, DE
29 May 2020